ORGANIC FORMULA

Number Energy as Portals to Self

By Ellen Brown Robinson
Author of The Joy Practice and A Good Mother

Organic Formula: Number Energy as Portals to Self

Ellen Brown Robinson

ISBN-13: 978-0578776262
ISBN-10: 0578776262

Published by Ellen Brown Robinson
Indianapolis, IN

Copyright © 2020 by Ellen Brown Robinson

All rights reserved. No part of this book may be reproduced without written permission from the publisher, except by a reviewer who may quote brief passages in a review; nor may any part of this book be reproduced, stored in a retrieval system or transmitted in any form or other without written permission from the publisher.

This book is manufactured in the United States of America.

Design/Layout: Andrew Brown
Artist: Ellen Brown Robinson

Special Thanks

Andrew Brown

> A portal is a doorway.

The number energies serve as portals. Portals to the Self. And these number energies are available moment to moment, as us. This is the pure potential that is available. Each person, me for me and you for you, will experience the portals of number energy in the way that is true for that person.

Some will skim the surface, some will get waist high, some will dive all the way in. There is no right way, there is no wrong way. The energies are here to be experienced and through this experiencing, open you to you.

This is not easy. It takes great guts to allow the extremes of the energies to show up. But when we do, because the energy is us, it means that we are allowing ourselves to show up in the greatest expression that we are.

Through the portals of number energy, we are taken into SELF. This raw experiencing is ALIVENESS. This is what it is to be truly human.

Organic:

Happening or developing naturally over time, without being forced or planned by anyone.

Formula:

A recipe or prescription.

Numerology, a Language of Love

The year I turned 40 (2008), was my first experience with numerology. My husband and I were in St. George, Utah for my birthday. On a whim, we attended a numerology workshop hosted by the place we were staying. I was mesmerized and I loved it. It was a different method than the one I use now, but it did not matter. I resonated so with the messages the numbers had for me. I played with the numbers for a while after our trip, but it wouldn't be until four years later, 2012, that I encountered numerology again. This time, it never let go.

Traditionally, numerology is known as the science of numbers. From my perspective and experience, it is a language of love, deeply encoded with light frequencies that have the power to evolve consciousness and free the soul.

Consciousness: that of which we are aware.
Soul: the truth of each being.

Yes. The essence of each number energy not only assists but exists to elevate awareness and reveal each individual's truest nature.

I remember feeling, both the first, and especially the second time I experienced number energy, like I had come home to myself. And this is the reason I am so passionate about numerology, or number energy, as I prefer to call it: I came to KNOW myself through the energy vibrations of the numbers.

I do not expect that you or anyone else will have the exact experience that I have had and have with number energy. I don't share this writing for you to "get" anything or to learn how to do or be something you aren't already. I have no interest in you being like me. What I have an interest in is me being me and you being you.

It's why we are here, to live our way to the truth that we are. Each individual is uniquely equipped for this. This unique equipping is my and your organic formula.

There is power in the beautiful language that is number energy. A power that has the potential to reveal the truth and bring wholeness. And I simply have no choice – I must share it with you.

The Power of Number Energy: Portals to Self

As I began to work with number energy, I learned the science, what the numbers mean, and the art, how to read a chart. And as I've lived my own life, I've come to understand that there is a third aspect to number energy, beyond the science and the art.

This third aspect is the energetic and transformational potential, that of evolving consciousness and freeing the soul. And the fact that the experiencing of each number energy serves as a portal to our truest nature. This experiencing happens moment to moment, as we live our lives.

As portals, each number energy, One through Nine, is a doorway into a yet to be known aspect of the Self. Availing ourselves to the full spectrum of experience within each number essence, we come to know these essences as inherent. Yes. In a very real way, the energy of numbers has the potential to carry us home to ourselves.

You do not have to look for a portal or have a special day to experience the opportunities that exist with a portal. Every human is a portal. You, me, and all, living our lives, is the portal to each person's essence.

Within this transformational power of number energy lies the pure potential for embodiment of our true nature.

The pure possibility is this:

Through the portal of ONE we become the CREATIVITY we ARE.

Through the portal of TWO we become the HARMONY we ARE.

Through the portal of THREE we become the EXPRESSION we ARE.

Through the portal of FOUR we become the SECURITY we ARE.

Through the portal of FIVE we become the FREEDOM we ARE.

Through the portal of SIX we become the RESPONSIBILITY we ARE.

Through the portal of SEVEN we become the TRUST we ARE.

Through the portal of EIGHT we become the VALUE we ARE.

Through the portal of NINE we become the WISDOM we ARE.

To be enlightened means to see clearly – to shed light on what we previously could not see. Carl Jung said, "One does not become enlightened by imagining figures of light, but by making the darkness conscious. The later procedure, however, is disagreeable and therefore not popular."

The same is true regarding the number essences, which are akin to archetype energies. The transformation happens to the extent that we are willing to meet ALL aspects of the Self. This is not easy as it requires meeting both the light and dark. The good and bad. The sunshine and the shadow. However, the more fearless we can be in allowing the full spectrum of ourselves to be, the more room for our souls to reveal themselves to us and live life as the Joy we are.

Number energy is in, and around us, at all times. Each letter of the alphabet resonates with one of the number essences. Literally, this writing is encoded and is an energy transmission. As we live our lives, number energy unlocks, activates, de-activates and reactivates within us, as us.

This unlocking has the power to free the truth of who one is from underneath layers of conditioning that so many individuals carry.

There is no trick or anything one must do. Each human being's unique energy code or organic formula provides everything needed to live our truest lives.

Organic Formula

Every individual comes to the planet with an energetic blueprint. This blueprint is that individual's organic formula. We can read this energetic blueprint using the date of birth and the name given at birth.

Each human's organic formula contains everything needed to live that human's truest life. In fact, our blueprint energies are soul-selected based upon that soul's desired experience and evolution in this lifetime.

Our organic formula or energy blueprint is comprised of a combination of number essences. The five core essences are known as the lifepath, motivation, personality, privilege and reality.

Additionally, each person's life is separated into four distinct phases that are each governed by number essences called conditions or pinnacles as well as challenges.

Finally, from the name as it appears on the certificate of birth, there are nine planes of expression, karmic debit and karmic accumulation energies.

We, as energy beings, came to planet earth to live these energies fully. However, once birthed, each human begins to take on the beliefs, ideas, and expectations of the collective consciousness. This is the conditioning of our lives and serves as a barrier between each human and their organic formula. Interestingly, embedded in each human's organic formula are the energetic codes necessary and capable of breaking each human of this very conditioning.

The Good Program

The conditioning of life, governed by the collective consciousness, is run like a program. I call this phenomenon, The Good Program. The exact nature of The Good Program is shaped by many external influences including one's culture, family, friends, religion, education, and more. As an overarching theme, however, The Good Program dictates that there are "good" and "appropriate" behaviors as well as "bad" and "inappropriate" behaviors. The Good Program uses shame and guilt, mostly, to keep its participants in line.

Shame is feeling bad for who one is. Guilt is feeling bad for what one does. Humans in general do not want to be thought of or think of themselves as bad, nor that they have done something bad. And thus, The Good Program keeps running.

The Good Program has hijacked, unwittingly for most humans, each being's organic formula. This, the living of one's life as that one's own essence - freely expressing one's natural life force.

This programming has the mass collective participating habitually and mostly unconsciously in a repetitive loop. The movie The Truman Show exemplifies this conditioning. Truman, played by Jim Carrey, must ultimately decide between accepting the artificial world he knows, or venturing into the unknown in pursuit of truth. Ultimately, this is what we must all decide.

And as each being wakes up to the artificial in their own lives, and this happens moment to moment, the question for each being is: do I choose my truth or do I continue to be a part of the programming. This unfolds in divine sequence for each being.

The conditioning of our lives conceals the truth of our lives until it doesn't.

Some humans are designed to live their way out of this conditioning, to break free of the conditioning that holds them. Other humans are designed to live in the conditioning - some happily, some miserably and many numb to it all.

When we live life, as I did for so long, according to The Good Program - how we think we should behave based on societal, cultural, familial, religious and even spiritual norms that are not true for us - we create a false self and from that, a false life. This falsity is toxic.

What I know is that when I allow myself to express who I am, uninhibited by fear, this is freedom. This is the truth of who I am. Before my truth revealed itself completely, I lived a pretend life. I mean, it was real, but it was not my true life. My pretending had become my way of being. No one knew that I was pretending. I didn't even know. I was too busy trying to be good.

The good girl. The good mom. The good daughter. The good friend. The good wife. The good employee. The good Catholic. Again, this idea of being good is fed by society – the group consciousness. And for the longest time I was all in with the group. My need to serve the group consciousness had me living a lie and carrying the lie got heavier and heavier. Eventually, I was able to live my way through the layers of falseness.

Our organic formula is always there asking, WHAT DO YOU (truly) WANT? This question may lie so deeply underneath the layers of conditioning that some may never hear it. For others, it's time.

Most humans are still running some level of The Good

Program. However, upon this writing in September 2020, we are at the beginning of a sped-up process of shedding this conditioning.

This is your Life. You get to choose or not choose what you do and do not do and with what you agree and disagree. Those things in your life that you believe are have-tos - those things are real until they are not. It is one's belief about something that makes it real for that person. Many hold on to beliefs that are no longer real for them, even when it hurts them, because the need to be pleasing to others and viewed as good, is stronger than taking responsibility for one's life.

This responsibility is the truth.

How Number Energy Works

Reading energy and reading numbers is the same thing. So, when a person comes to me for a number reading, it is really an energy reading. Each number carries with it a vibration and a meaning. There is logic in the numbers as they always mean what they mean; however, there are varying frequencies within each number essence.

Numerology is the language used to decode these frequencies as well as assist each being in the fine tuning of these frequencies. An individual's highest frequency is the one aligned with the truth of who they are – the essence of that person. One's essence is congruent with one's soul.

We are not born being our highest frequency. This is the point and purpose of life – to become our essence – to become who we truly are. The only way we can legit do this is by allowing the full expression of our life to occur.

This may seem like a simple statement. However, it is not easy to do because of the conditioning laying on top of our highest or most true frequency. The conditioning dims and oftentimes completely blots out our truest frequency. Our truest frequency is aligned with our greatest good and highest joy.

Number energy invites us to explore the vastness of the gifts that each number essence offers. This exploration challenges our set of conditioned beliefs. And, because it can be so challenging, many people end up editing the expression of their soul – who they truly are – trading in their truth for external ideas of who and what they and their life should be.

The truth of the soul is never convenient. It takes a brave

human to relish in and receive the full bounty of each number energy's potential. It is not as much a mental learning as it is a receiving of the divine gifts that we already are. It is with this receiving that comes a birthing into greater awareness and aliveness of the soul.

As we decide to live boldly, moment to moment, we begin to meet our conditioned self, head on. Experiencing our life directly, the conditioning begins to break up and have less of a hold on us.

There is nothing to do. Receiving life as it is happening is transformative fire and is your power.

Each number energy's unique essence is representative of who we are inherently. And it takes our human selves to unlock these gifts. Our experience as humans is the very catalyst that brings us to our true Self – the soul. This is a process of Integration – of coming into the wholeness of who we are.

Sometimes we cannot understand something with our logic. In fact, we are in a time and only growing more so, where logic can bog us down. Maybe you are experiencing this. But we have other ways of connecting to these powerful number frequencies - we can do so through the body (physical), heart (emotion), and the soul (spirit).

This is happening. We can trust this.

Number Energy and its Connection to Wholeness

The essence that we are is our truth. And this truth is wholeness. Wholeness does not mean positive or happy all the time. There is really no way to define wholeness except that wholeness is real. And realness is subjective to the person. Realness can be angry, frustrated and annoyed just as it can be happy, kind and serene.

Wholeness allows the Self to show up. No. Matter. What. And this is key: there is no conditioning cloaking it, meaning there is no shame or guilt attached to whatever is being thought or felt or experienced.

The difference between the false (fractured) self and the true (whole) Self is that the false self reacts in fear to guard its wound. This reaction can be to suppress the feelings, push them outward or both.

The whole Self responds in love because there is no longer anything to guard or fear. And love can be angry, frustrated or annoyed. Love is not absent these things. It's that the response is pure from one's wholeness. All falseness has been absorbed.

It's part of our conditioned self to live as if life is an idea – something outside of us. When we cease to live as if life is an idea outside of us, we are free to fully receive life as it is, as us. Number energy offers a framework for the transformational process of coming into the wholeness of Self.

It's Not Simple

Self-control is a mind fuck. This idea that proliferates our society that we can, are meant to, and are rewarded for, controlling the Self. It is true, as a society we value self-control. More than that, we lift it up as a virtue. Like so much, this value is fear-driven. Fear is the hidden engine of the group consciousness.

As a collective consciousness, we've set up an entire system of beliefs based on the importance of controlling the Self and how doing so makes us good, right and perfect. This need to control Self operates effortlessly and quietly. It shows up in a million different ways from the top levels of government, to the classroom, the boardroom, the therapy office, the yoga studio and the suburban living room.

This need to control the Self is primal because, deeply, it's about value and safety. The mind says, if I can be refrained in my emotions, if I'm disciplined enough in my exercise, if I train my mind just so, this means I am enough, valuable, and, therefore, safe.

This need to control blots out joy. Deeply, we are joy. Self-control blots out the Self. It is the trappings of the conditioned mind that does this. This conditioning that keeps us chained.

But these are simply ideas. Ideas that don't have to come along with us unless we want them to.

Number Energy, Zero and 1-9,
As Portals to Self

ZERO: Pure Potential

It's important to talk about Zero first because Zero is from where everything – literally, every thing – springs.

Zero is different than the other number essences. Zero is the mamba juice. Zero holds all the potential for each of the number essences, One through Nine.

When you take a look at 0, we see that it appears empty. But the beauty of Zero is that it can also be tremendously full. Zero is forever present. The energy of Zero was here before anything else was.

For people who believe in God, Zero is the energy of God. For people who believe in energy, Zero is pure energy. For people that believe in magic, Zero is magic. For people who believe in something but don't know what that is, Zero is simply the source.

The Zero exists as us.

Zero vibrates with the unmanifest - that which has not made its way into physical form because it has not even been thought of yet!

Zero is the wellspring. The place from which everything is made. I once said to my beautiful son Miles, "Everything is made up." And he looked at me and said, "No mommy, everything is made." Indeed. Everything is made from the Zero energy.

You do not have to believe in the idea that anything is possible. Because the Zero makes everything possible. Even when you don't believe it. Zero always exists as pure potential.

Zero is limitless. It is the pot that we dip our hand into to retrieve the fairy dust. Without Zero, nothing would be possible. Zero is a catalyst, bringing what was once not seen, into being on the physical plane. Ground Zero is truly the space from which reality manifests.

The Zero brings with it special gifts of strength, intuition, sensitivity and expression.

When a Zero appears in one's numerological birth chart, it can be a time of intense challenge or blessing and probably both. It is definitely an indication that truly anything is possible during this time. Often, Zero showing up in a person's chart is a call to step up and do something extraordinary for humankind. This will not be out of obligation, but out of pure love, integrity and truth. Or not. The unfoldment of each being is in perfect time. Always.

The Zero does not have a spectrum of experience the way that the other numbers, One through Nine, do. So how do we engage Zero energy? This is where the number One comes into play. The Zero energy needs the One energy to engage it and begin the creation process.

One Energy Experienced is the Portal to the Creativity we ARE

One is the birthplace of the Self.

The amazing thing about number energy is that at a deep and cosmic level, embedded within it, is the transformative purpose of supporting each human in becoming who they truly are, the natural Self. And we do this by experiencing each number's energy.

The divine gift of One is creativity. Creativity is who we are inherently. And it is the experiencing of the entire spectrum of One energy that is the alchemy to creativity as the Self.

Becoming conscious of the creativity we are is everything. As humans we are always creating using the energy that is us. The creative process happens one of two ways: consciously or unconsciously.

When we create consciously, we are aware of the thoughts we are choosing to think.

When we create unconsciously, we are thinking thoughts of which we are not aware. In effect, we are giving away our ability for free thought.

If you are not sure whether you are creating consciously or unconsciously, simply ask yourself: What is it that I WANT?

What a person wants requires a thought, idea or vision about that want. This vision is literally the One energy at play.

The energy of One is the starter energy. One starts a conversation, starts a relationship, starts a project. And in its most broad application, One energy is the seed of the Self. Yes. You as a human being started as a thought.

The One, as us, is creativity. Simply notice how it flows or doesn't flow. How it feels when it flows. How it feels when it does not flow. Creativity as us, simply wants to flow. Ideas. Innovation. Leading us into the great adventure that is us.

One, as an essence, has no other reference for the other energies because they literally have not been born yet. Think about that. Put up one finger. See it there by itself? One is the beginning of everything, the leader, the trailblazer, the pioneer.

One being the first, this energy sometimes brings with it a feeling of uncertainty on one end of the spectrum. And on the other end a feeling of ultra-certainty. The allowance of both experiences is the portal to the creativity that we are.

Do you know people who self-deflate or self-inflate or both? Have you experienced a bully in your life or perhaps you have been the bully? These experiences of self-deflation/self-inflation and being the bullied/bully are also the One portal doing what it does. All of it, the experience of One energy, and all of it, a pathway to the Self.

The One energy is necessary. However, One was never meant to stick around.

Creativity, the One, wants to throw shit against the wall to see what sticks. But as a society we've made what sticks a success and what doesn't stick a failure.

Creativity, the One, doesn't care about sticking or not sticking. Sometimes things stick and sometimes they don't. It's that simple. Creativity's job is simply to start.

The transformative fire of the One energy dares us to think for ourselves – to try something new – start something – decide something – freely choosing new thoughts – this is One – this is creativity. And it is us.

Two Energy Experienced is the Portal to the Harmony we ARE

Two is the soil that receives the Self (the One energy).

Two energy is feminine by nature. It is of the heart. It is love. And relationships are the catalyst.

Relationships with others show up in our lives to reflect the Self to the Self. This can be scary because acknowledging the Self in relationships changes relationships.

So instead of acknowledging the Self, many project, which is also consistent with Two energy. Projection is when our relationships show us something about ourselves that we don't want to see or accept. And in response, we project it onto the person with whom we are in relationship.

And there is yet a third option consistent with Two energy. And that is when the Self sees an aspect of the Self that wants to be acknowledged, and neither acknowledges nor projects, and instead mutes that aspect of Self. This is not sustainable.

It is not so much a mental learning as it is an unfolding of experience. The Two journey takes us from the experience of abandonment on one end of the spectrum all the way over to the other side where we visit rejection. This shows up in relationships until we become aware that our greatest deception is when we reject and abandon our own Self.

When we look to our relationships to do something for us that we really need to do for ourselves first, we experience conflict and stress. For instance, most every human, wants, needs and craves connection. But no relationship can give us this connection as a replacement for our own sense of connection to Self.

This transformational fire of evolution cannot be escaped or avoided. This journey is full and alive, and it is heartbreaking. And is necessary to a full manifestation of Harmony - the ultimate gift of Two energy.

The Two energy of peace and harmony is inherent in each being. But as humans, we are conditioned to believe that peace and harmony are a result of everyone around us being happy and pleased. This works for a time, but eventually the full experience of Two will arrive to deliver each human to the harmony of her own being. Often this shows up as conflict in relationships. Conflict stemming from choosing to honor what the Self needs. The following quote by Jane Fonda illustrates what I am talking about:

> "Up until my sixties, I was to an extent, defined by the men in my life. I was brought up to please. I wanted my father to love me so I would turn myself into a pretzel to be what he wanted me to be, not necessarily what I already was. It took me getting into my sixties, and then I began to become who I was supposed to be all along."
>
> – Jane Fonda, 2018

When I started to go through, as my therapist at the time called it, my individuation process, it was a very uncertain time for me and my husband. When you are in relationship for a long time, as my husband and I, you move as a couple, decide as a couple, it even feels like you share the same brain at times. It came to a point where I could not delineate where I ended, and my husband began.

This no longer felt good to me.

So, I started to make decisions from my truth instead of always bouncing everything off my husband. For instance, we worked out together. It seemed like an almost sacred thing we did. Together. I realized at some point that I wanted to do something different, I wanted to sign up for boxing classes. I remember at the time I did sign up for them, but I did not tell my husband until after the fact. It felt like I was betraying him. I knew his feelings would be hurt and I did not want to be the cause of his hurt feelings. I now see clearly that I was not betraying him at all. What I was doing was honoring my individual truth.

This has been the reality of couple-hood, that we adjust for our partners and they for us. But there is a new paradigm emerging around not just couple-hood, but all kinds of relationships and partnerships. It is possible to do something different.

As humans, when we operate from our individual truth, we organically become the harmony that we are – our insides are harmonious. From this authentic place, we create organic partnerships.

Thirteen years ago, I created some visions for my life. One was to be connected and free in all of my relationships. What I did not know at the time, was what that really meant – over the next decade I would learn to receive my own Self – be in relationship with me. This is the harmony of Two energy.

The relationship we have with ourselves is the first thing that matters, or nothing matters.

But it's part of the collective consciousness to need others to relate to us. On one end of the Two spectrum, we suffocate others with this need. On the opposite end we push others away – which says, I don't need you. These experiences eventually deliver us to the sweetness of relating to our own Self.

You know what you need to take care of you. The little things are as important at the big things. Allowing yourself to feel your feelings and think all your thoughts – this is you receiving you. It seems small but it is huge. Groundbreaking. Breaking the layers of conditioning free.

You may be wondering how do I do that? How do I receive myself? There is no prescribed formula, only the organic formula of you, being in and experiencing each moment. This is you receiving YOU.

I DON'T WANT TO. Such a simple statement, we might overlook its power. We might even laugh at this statement or say some snarky comment back to our child when they say this about something they don't want to do.

I WANT TO. Also. A damn powerful statement. Acknowledging what we don't want and acknowledging what we do want, is loving the Self ... receiving the Self that we are. This is the Two energy nurturing the One energy – YOU!

Receiving the thoughts and feelings that come from our nature is badass. This is how we begin to learn about our preferences. Again, social, cultural and familial conditioning encourages group thinking. I remember the first time I heard the phrase: You get what you get so don't throw a fit. This is the collective consciousness at work saying: you may not want what you want, nor do you get to feel any kind of way about it.

However, when we can begin to know what our preferences are, this is everything - our preferences give us clues into loving ourselves...into being the love that we are.

Relating to ourselves, we no longer have to out-source that job. This is true harmony and in this truth our relationships become truer and freer.

It is human to look to the other in our relationships for answers, permission, love. But the Two that is you will have nothing of that for the other is simply a mirror. We are our answer. Only we can give ourselves permission. We, ourselves, are the source of the purest love.

And yes. We bring in relationships to learn to love the Self. Loving the Self can feel quite vulnerable in our world where some of the conditioned beliefs include: "bite the bullet," "suck it up," and "put your game face on."

Eventually, the experience of Two energy will include setting boundaries. This is uncomfortable. It is uncomfortable because the nature of Two is extremely sensing. Two is the empath energy and as such, a person experiencing Two energy can feel other peoples' feelings. This person, carrying Two energy, must be willing to sit in the discomfort of displeasing another in order to gain their own sense of internal peace and harmony. This is the Two (YOU) learning to love itself (YOU).

Experiencing Two energy also means taking things personally. Taking something personally is taking something someone else says or does and putting it on our person. This does not feel good because it is not congruent with the harmony we are. Taking things personally is so painful.

Many people take things personally, never acknowledging the hurt they feel because they fear losing love. The Two need is a need to fill one's self up with others' love. It is human to want and need to be loved. But when we trade in the Self, the essence of who we are, to get this love, then we become sick with the need to be loved. This is not sustainable.

The Two energy is giving by nature. But this giving does not mean we have to delete the Self. On the contrary, when we receive the Self, we give of the Self in the highest way.

The emergent partnership paradigm of all kinds - lovers, friendships, business - is not about compromise or somehow tucking part of oneself away from view - rather, each person being the wholeness of who they are. As this happens, partnerships that were predicated on conditions drop away and partnerships based on harmony begin to take shape organically.

When we begin to say and do what is harmonious for us as opposed to how we are programmed, this will 100% guaranteed rock the boat. And. It is possible to break the conditioning of our lives. We are built for this. Each human, equipped with their organic formula, that supports each of us in being our most harmonious selves.

Three Energy Experienced is the Portal to the Expression we ARE

Three is the VOICE of the Self.

We've discussed the energy of One being the seed of the Self and the energy of Two being the soil that receives the Self. Three, then, is the expression of that communion. It is the butterfly breaking free of the chrysalis, the flower bursting forth from the bud and the baby being birthed.

Three exists to support each being in owning their emotional integrity, how one truly feels. And just as the other essences do, the Three energy exists along a spectrum of experience. The extremes of Three energy, under-feeling and over-feeling, keep the Self from feeling what it is really feeling - the truth of one's emotions.

Three energy is extremely sensitive. Three wants all of the credit, but none of the blame. Three's need is external validation, affirmation and approval. This need is insatiable, which makes it unsustainable.

Repression of expression is the root of anxiety and depression. Anxiety and depression are opposite ends of the Three spectrum of experience. Both anxiety and depression happen by attempting to contain overwhelm. They just feel very different.

When the Self is ready to own its emotional integrity - how the Self truly feels about a person, a situation, anything - everything changes. This is when life becomes real.

It's difficult. The societal conditioning trains that it is **not** okay to have our feelings, that we must manage and control our emotions. And so, we do this. Until we don't. Until we cannot manage or control one more minute. Allowing the Self to feel the truth of one's emotions is absolutely freeing.

And it can be terrifying for those who've lived their entire lives not feeling. Three energy helps each being break through the training in order to experience all that one is; one's truest expression.

When I say experience all that we are, I am talking about allowing our emotions to come to the surface to be felt and acknowledged. I understand that this goes against our mental and logical world.

Three is the energy of the child. Many people were not allowed to express as children or had to skip being a child and be the adult due to an emotionally, physically, or mentally absent parent. It is never too late to begin to allow our child energy to express. It is imperative for our growth and evolution, not only as individuals, but as a planet.

A couple of years ago I remember dropping off my daughter at her new school. She had switched schools mid-year during her eighth-grade year. After walking her to the door I got in my car. I was feeling a feeling I was unfamiliar with ... I realized it was overwhelm. What I did next is not what we are conditioned to do – I let the overwhelm come. I allowed my overwhelm a space to be. Just because we are adults does not mean we don't have feelings that need to be expressed. We do. And it is normal. And healthy.

Emotions exist to be felt, not analyzed, or picked apart or figured out.

As the voice of the Self, on one end, Three energy under-expresses and on the opposite end, over-expresses. Understated versus overstated. Three energy can show up as drama and hysteria or as people walking around zombified because they are frozen in their emotions. Both experiences serve as the portal to the expression that we are.

Three is also the addict energy. Think about this: Three energy invites us to feel – to be alive in our life. When a person is wholly experiencing the energy of Three, they have ups and downs and everything in between. Because life is ups and downs and everything in between.

As a society, we have conditioned ourselves away from feeling these ups and downs because the feelings are uncomfortable. We will do anything to get relief from these uncomfortable feelings. Hence, the addict energy. Whatever it is we are addicted to: alcohol, food, exercising, being good, making ourselves valuable, being a bully, work, being right, sex, pleasing others, anger and so much more – these are things we use to get out of the feeling we are in.

But Three will keep tracking us down. Three's desire? That we own our emotional integrity – the truth of how we feel. It is human to avoid this. Because owning our emotional integrity means our life changes. It can also be scary because it can feel out of control.

Becoming whole in the expression we are means we must see, hear and affirm our own self. Our own voice. Our own life. It does not mean that others can't acknowledge and affirm us. The difference is, in our wholeness, we don't need outside affirmation to feel good about ourselves.

In our wholeness we express freely.

Four Energy Experienced is the Portal to the Security we ARE

The Four energy is Safety as the Self.

As energy beings, we literally are our own security system. And through our human experience we have the power to embody the security we are. This is a big picture perspective and it can take lifetimes to fully realize security, a feeling of safeness, within our being.

Experiencing Four energy includes the dynamics of practicality, logic, work, order, structure, process. Four energy is the glue that holds it all together. Four energy is habits and routines. Four is structural and foundational. Four is planful. Four is when we roll up our sleeves and get to work. Four can be frugal. Four gets the job done. All of these, attributes of Four energy, designed to one end, security - an attempt to feel safe and in control of one's life and circumstances.

The Four energy is for us to experience, from one end of the spectrum, which is no order or plans to the opposite end of the spectrum that includes so many plans and structure that life is rigid. Additionally, the person we call a bum on one end of the spectrum and the other end is the person we call a workaholic. Each extreme and everything in between, simply experiences, the portal, to the security we are.

Four energy has the tendency to dig deep in the quest for one's own self-security. Under the umbrella of the Four experience is our nuclear family – the one we grew up with.

We move in our lives believing certain truths and behaving in certain ways that stem from our experiences with our nuclear families. For many these beliefs and ideas provide a great source of comfort and security.

In theory, our nuclear family is our safety net – our pod. In practice, many do not experience safety within their nuclear families. Instead, many experience the opposite, including physical, emotional and psychological harm. These experiences, too, a portal designed by us, for us, to ultimately take us into the security that we are.

It is a primal need of humans to feel safe. But it is an error to believe that the answer to our safety and security somehow lives outside of us. On the contrary, when we are fully grounded in our physical home, our bodies, this is the inherent security that is available to all of us.

But we must live our way to the space of realizing (making real) this in our bodies. We must go through the process of trying to access this safety through external means. It is the allowance of the extremes that eventually reveals the security that is inherent to our very nature.

Traditionally, Four is the worker and the doer energy. And. Sometimes the most powerful thing we can ever do is be present to our own experience – our own pain, our own joy, our own anger, our own guilt, our own excitement. Being present to all of it, we are present to our own Self. *Our presence is as grounded as it gets, bringing our experience into the body as the body.*

Our bodies are our personal energy systems and hold our greatest truths. As such, they are our most reliable source of information. Our bodies are receptors of information transmitted from the soul and heart as well as external messages.

Fully in each moment, when we allow our bodies to experience what is happening in real time, we access the security that is inherent in our being. We ground into our own essence. Our own Earthly Matter.

Four is foundational, girding us for what's next: CHANGE.

Five Energy Experienced is the Portal to the Freedom we ARE

The Five energy is Freedom as the Self.

Experiencing the extremes of each number's energy spectrum is the portal to being the divinity we are, in Five's case, freedom. The kind of freedom I'm talking about is freedom in one's own experience.

Five resonates with experimentation, which includes an under-doing or lack of experimentation on one end and an over-doing or proliferation of experimentation on the other end. Five simply wants to explore and experience all of what life has to offer through all of the senses.

Like Four energy, Five is representative of the physical body. Unlike Four energy, which is physically strong, Five energy is physically restless.

When there is a Five in someone's number chart, this indicates change. This change could look any number of ways, but it always shows up as some sort of upheaval. Five energy is chaotic and restless, designed to take whoever is experiencing it, out of their comfort zone. Five exists to ensure we do not get stuck in a rut.

Five energy ensures there will be lots to spontaneously experience. Five energy invites risk, adventure and movement. Five is at its most benign, an energy of transition, and at its most intense, truly transformational.

The experience of Five is sandwiched between Four and Six, making Five the bridge from the experience of security (4) to the experience of responsibility (6).

We feel safe in the security of Four and then, BAM, Five comes along with all of its CHANGE. And although it can feel like WTF?!, Five energy serves to lift everything up that is not nailed down ensuring that we do not stay in the rigidity and control that Four energy can get us into.

In its chaos, Five does what it does best and that is: it takes a bite of us, chews us up and spits us out. This is transformation. After the Five energy has its way with us, we are the same, yet we are different. We are more of who we are. This transformation is freedom.

What do you need to do to feel free within yourself? What experiences are you being called to - body, mind, heart and soul? There is always more of the Self to free.

Five paves the way for the experience of Six, which gets us clear on the truth of the heart.

Six Energy Experienced is the Portal to the Responsibility We ARE

Six takes us into the truth of the heart.

Six energy exists to support each being in responding truthfully in terms of how we are living our lives – the choices we make in our everyday lives.

Experiencing the energy of Six requires living our way through the guilt, martyrdom, victimhood, perfectionism and right-ness that are part of obligation. This living through opens the responsibility we are.

As humans we often use these words interchangeably, obligation and responsibility. But they are very different. One is born out of victim energy – a belief that my life happens to me – and one springs from empowerment energy – I make my life through my choices.

It is necessary to allow the guilt associated with Six in order to get to the heart truth. This is the hard part. It is part of The Good Program to be motivated by guilt. Guilt comes from obligation. Obligation is the have-tos, shoulds and ought-tos. According to The Good Program, this is called service. But this is not the truth. When we are motivated by our true response - what we must do because our heart says so, this is responsibility. This responsibility that we are, our greatest service.

Obligation is part of our fractured self – the lie that covers our truth. Obligation must be experienced mentally, physically and emotionally in order to integrate it. This is not easy, but we are built for it. The conditioning of our lives assists us with this process. This conditioning includes our cultural, familial, religious and other agreements. These group agreements exist as an energy web that holds that group together. This web is the group consciousness. This group consciousness is where the unconscious agreements of belonging to the group lie.

It is during our natural evolution - the embodying of our soul - that we begin to notice these unconscious group agreements. I grew up Catholic and in 2008 at 40-years-old, I attended my last church service. I stopped mid-sentence while reciting one of the Catholic prayers. I realized in that moment that I did not know what I was saying and that I was reciting it because that's what I always did. The truth for me was that Catholicism no longer felt good to me. It was time for me to move away from the church.

This was a big thing at the time, but it happens in seemingly small ways too. Being a part of a neighborhood book club and going every week when we really don't want to and would rather be home in our pajamas. I still remember the day that I sent an email to one of these groups in my own neighborhood with the words: TAKE ME OFF THE EMAIL LIST. It took me three years to get to the place where I could send that email.

What happens when we go along with these agreements that are no longer true for us is that we betray the truth of our heart. This creates anxiety and unease in the body. We do this in order to belong and to be liked. I did. And we are not conscious of this until we are. This is not to say do not be part of groups. What I am saying is there is a consciousness that any group has in common and this consciousness is an animal unto itself. Be aware. And notice how you feel in the group and when you are interacting with the group.

When we decide that we no longer align with the agreements of our lives, whatever they may be, this is when things begin to change. When we have the courage to say NO to a group agreement that is no longer true for us, this impacts our community circle.

Each time we make the choice in support of our truth versus how we've been conditioned, this is a HUGE thing. It is the very act of making a different choice that is where the transformation of evolution happens.

This is the joy that comes from freedom – the freedom to truly be ourselves. Whenever we are being truly who we are from our essence - our soul - this is what inspires. No additional effort required. And know, disrupting and disturbing are also forms of inspiring.

I remember the day, my husband said to me, "You're a disruptor." At first, I took offense. My offense was part of my own social conditioning. I now know the importance of disrupting and disturbing the status quo of our lives.

The conditioning of the Six energy experience wants us to stay within the lines and reply, same old, same old, when someone asks how we are doing. The truth of the heart will have nothing of this. This truth shatters the mold of our conditioning.

The opposite of responsibility is perfectionism. The Six energy of responsibility gets us clear on the truth of the heart - one's truest response - RESPONSE-ability. Actual responsibility is love (the heart) in action. Responsibility is being alive in the heart.

Perfectionism is the opposite of this. Perfectionism exists as an idea or group of ideas about what one should do, how things should look - it is all about perception. What things look like. Again, the idea of something versus the truth of what is real. Perfectionism is being dead in the heart.

Every realization of your truth is important and valid. The big and the small. Only you know the truth of your heart. And you will know it when you know it.

And it is no one's fault, and everyone is complicit. Perfectionism is supported by the group consciousness - the collective programming and patterning that covers up what is real and true.

There are layers upon layers upon layers of this conditioning. And the destruction of this conditioning is happening. More and more people are and will be waking up to the falseness that is their life. The untruths that they are living - again, this will represent in the seemingly small things as well as the seemingly big things. And everything is big.

Every WAKING UP moment serves to bring each human HOME to their own HEART.

It's all necessary for us to ultimately land in the center of our Hearts - what we must do, not because we think we should or ought to or someone else thinks we should or ought to, but because our heart tells us we must.

Seven Experienced is the Portal to the Trust We ARE

Seven is self-knowing.

Like each of the number essences, the energy of Seven exists to support humanity. As we live, we uncover the truth of who we are and remember our natural essence. Specifically, Seven energy assists us on our human journey in becoming the Trust that we ARE.

Somewhere in the midst of this, the Seven experience invites that we trust the Self. Trusting the Self does not require that one know it all. Or that one has all the answers. Trusting the Self and not knowing it all can co-exist. Both can be true. We don't have to wait until we know every drop of everything to be the trust that we are in the moment.

Seven energy experiences include skepticism and paranoia on one end of the spectrum and blind faith and gullibility on the opposite end. Also, seeking outside of itself for all the answers versus being a know it all.

Faith. Believing before we can see what is coming. This is the Seven energy. Skepticism. Not believing anything until it's proven. This, too, is the energy of Seven.

Seven is the observer energy. It is introspective and from this introspection comes clarity. And because it's experienced on a spectrum, Seven energy can also be extremely thought-focused. So many thoughts that paralysis of the mind sets in. And then there is absolutely no clarity.

Do you know people that pride themselves on being a seeker - those that seek for the answer outside of themselves? I sought outside of myself for the longest time. I was an avid reader. I went to multiple workshops and saw many a spiritual healer. And all of this was perfect and purposeful. I had to walk this journey in order to one day realize what I had been seeking was ME.

Yes, the Seven energy takes each being into his/her own knowing. But the experience of Seven is such that we must seek outside of the Self first. Ultimately, the experience will lead back to the Self.

All of these experiences are the Seven energy: intellectual, scientific, skeptical, mystical, spiritual, gullible, fearful, faithful, afraid, trusting, knowing everything, knowing nothing, seeking outside of the self, pure presence, thoughts clogging up the brain ... all of this to take us into the essence of Trust that we are.

It is so much more than trusting the Self. It is being the trust that we are. Embodying our own essence of trust, we become the intuition we are. Intuition is the ability to understand something immediately, without the need for conscious reasoning. Yes. We block our own intuition with our intellect. This. Is. The. Spectrum. Of. Seven. And as we live the spectrum, we naturally become the trust that we are.

It's frustrating, I know. We want clarity now. But the only way to clear the path is to walk that path - to live our way to our own knowing.

As mentioned, the Seven can be highly intellectual on one end of the spectrum and highly spiritual on the other end of the spectrum. Often these two elements combine to create spiritual dogma: the idea that there is only one way to be spiritual.

Many people carrying Seven energy leave traditional religions because of the dogma only to pick up a new set of dogma such as yoga, meditation, or mantra-saying. This is not to say don't do these things. Quite the opposite. It's all part of the journey of coming into your own knowing and your own truth.

The Seven energy can have the Self wanting to know so badly that it ignores what it knows inherently and listens to someone outside of the Self because it's a convenient truth. The Self forgoing its own knowing, handing it over to someone else.

This is when the know it all steps up to the plate. The know it all is also the Seven energy at work. The know it all thinks she is right above all others. The know it all thinks she knows for other people. The know it all thinks it's her responsibility to show others the way.

But the thing is, we know what we know when we know it. And what we come to know is for our own Self. Ultimately each human must find their own way to the center of the Self.

For all of her knowing, the know it all does not know herself. The know it all is driven by fear. The fear of actually knowing herself and that her real self will be revealed. The know it all does not know that she lives in fear.

Eventually, people in the life of the know it all start to come into their own knowing of self and the reliance on the know it all becomes less and less. This is when the know it all must also face herself. Taking responsibility for our own knowing, opens us to the trust that we are.

As humans, we live most of our lives asleep to the Self. Seven takes us on a journey into the Self and assists the Self in knowing the Self.

This is the waking up.

Eight Energy Experienced is the Portal to the Value We ARE

Eight is Value as the Self.

Each being embodied in their Eight divinity is the essence of their own being. What does this mean, to be our essence? You, me, all, are energy. When we completely own our energy, we enact it, we plug into the Self. There is nothing external about real power. We are this real power and this real power is our value.

The Eight energy brings experiences such as run-ins with authority figures, being highly competitive, not feeling worthy, a feeling of being better than others and needing to win at all costs, to name a few. It is mental and masculine energy that wants to be in control and in charge. This is all part of the great spectrum of the Eight energy, delivering us to the power that we are, to fully animate our inner authority.

When a person feels powerless in their life, this is the Eight energy at work. What does this powerlessness feel like? It feels like insignificance, unworthiness, scarcity. This powerlessness is a portal. But as humans, we tend to avoid feelings that don't feel good. We try to go around.

In the case of the Eight energy, the person that feels powerless will attempt to dominate and control others or try to convince others that they are valuable. Both tactics are consistent with manipulation, which is a manifestation of the Eight energy.

And both tactics provide a false sense of power and value and are not sustainable. Eventually, the person will have no other recourse then to enter the portal of powerlessness. The alchemy occurs as one traverses the portal, experiencing head-on, feelings they once avoided. In doing so, this person embodies their own value, their power.

Eight's job is to insist that we take ownership of our lives - that we step into our personal power. Eight energy gives us the gumption to stand straighter and taller and act in accordance with our inner authority.

The Eight energy is the potential for Self-Mastery. As masters of the Self, we are self-sovereign. She that is self-sovereign does not need to prove anything. She has received the power that she is. She exudes power by simply being. Being is her power.

The space of embodiment, of enactment of one's life force, of animating one's own essence, must be lived to. Yes, intellectually, one may understand. But again. This happens in the body as each being lives their life.

Deeply, the energy of Eight is about value.

As humans, we tend to see external accomplishments, such as titles, relationship connections with the right people, living in certain neighborhoods, awards, having a certain amount of money, as evidence of our value. These things are what they are, but they don't make us valuable. They don't give us our value. My value, your value - it's inherent. It's already there. Perhaps it's asleep.

And it's a choice every single moment to wake up to the value that we are.

Eight invites action that empowers our lives. Eight says: Put your crown on and take dominion over your own energy and being.

Nine Energy Experienced is the Portal to the Wisdom We ARE

Nine Energy assists in letting go of what was to receive what is.

We don't show up as wise. We live our way to wise. Living our life is the portal that opens the Wisdom that we are.

When we get to Nine, we can look back and review the choices we've made. This may bring disappointment based on unfulfilled expectations. That's why Nine is the would of, could of, should of energy. If we would have known then, what we know now, we could have done something different, should have done something different…but we didn't know then what we know now.

The thing is, Nine energy is the end. We didn't know at the beginning that which we know now. Perhaps we would have made a different choice, perhaps not. But that is the gift of Nine energy - allowing the Self the space to live.

The magic of Nine is its organic journey to forgiveness & compassion, first and foremost of Self. In this way, the Nine energy asks that we simply let go and live. This living turns the key to open the wisdom that is inherent in our being. What served us before, no longer serves.

Nine is resonate with surrender. Surrender is really a type of receiving. It is the receiving of what is. It is the surrender to the resistance of what is so that we can receive the nourishment from it.

Nine energy represents completion and the emotion associated with Nine is grief. Grief is what we must go through to get to what's next. Grief is the price to be paid for wisdom. The level of Nine energy each being experiences is subjective to each being. Grief is personal.

This is the energy of Nine: show up and live your life. That's what it's for. For giving. Each being. Everything needed. To live her truest life. FOR GIVING: Experiences given for the purpose of opening the wisdom that is us.

Yes. The energy of forgiveness is in alignment with the essence of Nine. And forgiveness is not some idea outside of us. Forgiveness is you living your life and me living my life. No holds barred: free of restrictions or hampering conditions.

But we are human. And so we do live our lives restricted and hampered with conditions. This is what being human is.

Whereas One energy has no reference for the other number energies, Nine energy is made up of each of the other number energies. We couldn't get to Nine if we hadn't lived One through Eight. On our way to living our truest life, we get to move through the portals of each of the other energies and in so doing, become more of who we are.

One takes us into the Creativity we ARE. Two takes us into the Harmony we ARE. Three takes us into the Expression that we ARE. Four takes us into the Security that we ARE. Five takes us into the Freedom that we ARE. Six takes us into the Responsibility that we ARE. Seven takes us into the Trust that we ARE. And Eight takes us into the Value that we ARE.

Once we get to Nine, we can look back and see that who we once were is not who we are now. Even the physical construction of the number Nine, with One as the trunk and Zero on top, indicates that we must die to the Self (One) that we have known in order to open up to the unlimited possibility (Zero) of what could be.

This is not something that can be forced. Each being must live their way to this space. This naturally brings grief. Especially when we see that we were not living our truest life all along. But we did not know then what we know now. And this understanding of our own humanity brings compassion.

As grief, Nine guts us. Allowing this full gutting is the beauty of Nine. Allowing grief to do what it does, it strips us. It completely separates us from any false ideas about ourselves that are no longer true and that are holding us in old energy patterns.

This is Nine. Nine is the truth of the soul. It is our human self, living in the world as our soul self. This is integrity. And integrity is personal. Living our lives, opens us to the wisdom we are.

I was watching a new show a while ago and the main character said this line: "Knowledge is a rumor until it lives in the body. Which means, you don't really know something until your body knows it."

This is so true. And how does the body come to know something? By living life. The Nine energy invites us to live and the living turns the key of wisdom and wisdom floods the body. And that is how we truly know it.

Because it is us. Wisdom is us.

BEING YOU; A REVOLUTIONARY ACT

Being who you are is the most revolutionary act there is.

There is no right or wrong way to be you. Simply however YOU do it. That's why it's revolutionary. Because no one is you like you are you.

As individual beings, we bring in everything we need - each interaction, encounter, happening, thought, feeling, relationship. Each of these experiences, interacting in divine sequence with your personal energy composition in the moment for your unique evolution.

Waking up to the LIFE that we are, is an unfoldment. It occurs in the little moments and the big moments. The still moments and the loud moments. The happy and the sad moments. All these moments made of life. The life of you and the life of me. And each being wakes up in perfect time according to each being's organic formula.

This is how we free ourselves. This is how we free others. This is how we free the world.

ARTWORK by Ellen Brown Robinson
In order of appearance

Organic Formula (Cover)
Ring of Fire (Zero)
Beginnings (One)
Eve (Two)
Drink with a Straw (Three)
Flattened (Four)
Kashmir (Five)
Love Knows No Bounds (Six)
Color of My Soul (Seven)
It's Time (Eight)
Joy Vibration (Nine)

www.ingramcontent.com/pod-product-compliance
Lightning Source LLC
Chambersburg PA
CBHW042338150426
43195CB00001B/35